Just for Laughs

GOOFY, NUTTY JOKES
ABOUT PARENTS AND TEACHERS

Julia Garstecki

BLACK
RABBIT
BOOKS

Hi Jinx is published by Black Rabbit Books
P.O. Box 3263, Mankato, Minnesota, 56002.
www.blackrabbitbooks.com
Copyright © 2018 Black Rabbit Books

Marysa Storm, editor; Michael Sellner, designer;
Omay Ayres, photo researcher

Library of Congress Cataloging-in-Publication Data
Names: Garstecki, Julia, author.
Title: Goofy, nutty jokes about parents and teachers /
by Julia Garstecki.
Description: Mankato, Minnesota : Black Rabbit Books, [2018] |
Series: Hi jinx. Just for laughs | Includes bibliographical
references and index.
Identifiers: LCCN 2017007249 (print) | LCCN 2017024096
(ebook) | ISBN 9781680723571 (e-book) | ISBN 9781680723274
(library binding)
Subjects: LCSH: Parents–Juvenile humor. | Teachers–Juvenile
humor. | Wit and humor, Juvenile.
Classification: LCC PN6231.P2 (ebook) | LCC PN6231.P2 G37
2018 (print) | DDC 818/.602–dc23
LC record available at https://lccn.loc.gov/2017007249

Printed in the United States. 9/18

Image Credits

Dreamstime: Dietmar Höpfl, 14 (wig); iStock: P-Scott, 9 (top); Shutterstock:
AmazeinDesign, 2–3, 16 (yawning pill); akarakingdoms, 20 (dog); Amornism,
13 (bookworm); anfisa focusova, 12 (bkgd); Angeliki Vel, 4 (sun); Arkadivna,
16 (bkgd); blambca, 10 (man, pan); chompoo, 6 (fart); Christos Georghiou, 19
(torn ppr); Cory Thoman, 11 (lightning), 14 (all but wig); Dario Sabljak, Cover
(science sketches), 11 (bkgd); Dennis Cox, 17 (closet); Ilya Chalyuk, 5 (marker
strokes), 6 (marker strokes), 16 (marker strokes), 20 (marker stroke); Jeff Morin,
1 (chalkboard, man), 6 (chalkboard, man), 13 (hook); kagankiris, 8 (lightbulb);
Katerina Davidenko, 4–5 (hill); Liron Peer, 20 (man); Lorelyn Medina, 16 (bottles);
Mangm srisukh stock photo, 17 (bkgd); Memo Angeles, Cover (man), 1 (pug), 6
(pug), 8 (teacher, kids), 9 (kids), 11 (man), 12 (people), 13 (people, desk), 18–19,
19 (woman, boy), 21 (scientist), 23 (bttm); newyear, 7 (web); opicobello, 10 (top
corner), 15 (marker strokes); Pasko Maksim, Back Cover (top), 12 (bttm), 23
(top), 24; Pitju, 7 (curl), 17 (curl), 21 (curl); Pushkin, 6 ("Pfff! cloud"); Ravital,
16 (pills); Ron Leishman, 8 (desk), 10 (bttm), 15 (girl, desk, bubble), 16 (man),
17 (treadmills, woman, boy, man), Teguh Mujiono, 15 (background); totallypic,
15 (arrow); Tueris, 9 (marker strokes); Valerie Bodnar, 13 (sea bkgd); V_ctoria, 3
(bkgd); Vecster, 16 (tired pills' expressions); Vector Tradition SM, Cover (bkgd),
Back Cover (bkgd), 8 (light bulb face); Verzzh, 4 (boy, adult), 5; Zern Liew, Cover
(mints), 11 (mints), 21 (mints) Every effort has been made to contact copyright
holders for material reproduced in this book. Any omissions will be rectified in
subsequent printings if notice is given to the publisher.

CONTENTS

CHAPTER 1

All Work and
No Play?.............5

CHAPTER 2

Schooling Teachers...6

CHAPTER 3

Jokes about Parents
and Grandparents....16

CHAPTER 4

Get in on the Hi Jinx..20

Other Resources.........22

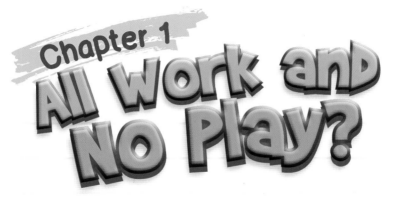

Chapter 1
All Work and No Play?

Teachers and parents can be so bossy! They are always giving out homework and chores. Maybe they're so bossy because they are in bad moods. Why not try telling them jokes to lighten their moods? If that doesn't work, you can at least make yourself laugh.

Chapter 2
Schooling Teachers

What do you call a teacher
who only farts after
students go home?

a private tooter

PFFF!

Why did the school fire Spider-Man
from teaching computer class?
*He kept trying to make a
worldwide web.*

Why didn't the
classroom have chairs?
*Because the teacher
told her students to
take their seats.*

Why did the teacher turn on the lights?
Because his class was so dim!

Teacher: Didn't I tell
you to stand at the
end of the line?
*Student: You did, but
somebody was already there.*

Why did the teacher wear sunglasses?

His students were so bright!

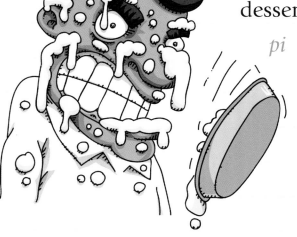

What do math teachers eat for dessert?

pi

Teacher: Craig, you know you can't sleep in my class.

Craig: Maybe if you weren't so loud, I could.

How do science teachers
keep their breath fresh?
They use experi-mints.

11

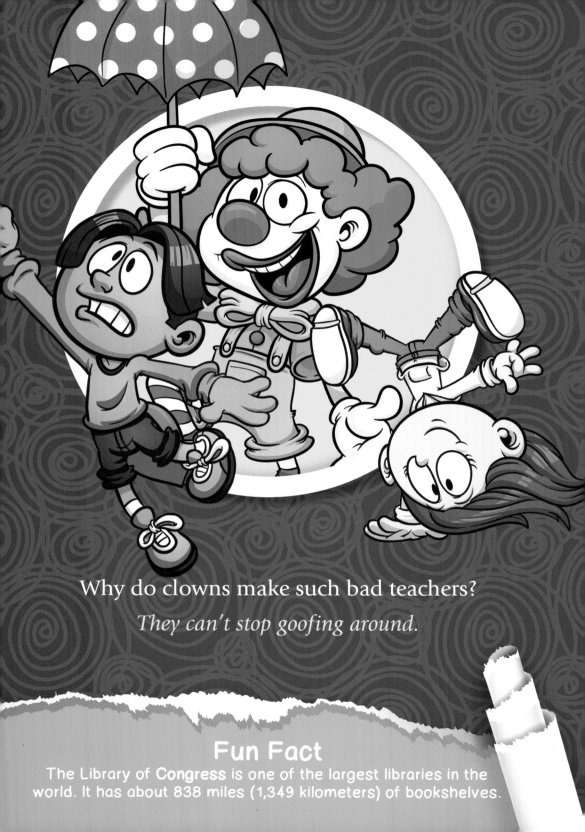

Why do clowns make such bad teachers?

They can't stop goofing around.

Fun Fact
The Library of Congress is one of the largest libraries in the world. It has about 838 miles (1,349 kilometers) of bookshelves.

What do librarians
use to go fishing?

bookworms

Student: I don't think I
deserve a zero on this test!

*Teacher: I agree, but that's the
lowest score I could give you.*

Social studies teacher: Where was the **Declaration** of Independence signed?

Student: At the bottom.

Why do most math teachers write **advice columns**?

Because they're good at solving problems.

Fun Fact
Some research suggests homework is actually bad for your health.
Too much homework can cause **stress** and **exhaustion**!

Chapter 3
Jokes about Parents and Grandparents

Why did the grandpa tiptoe
past the medicine cabinet?

He didn't want to wake his sleeping pills.

Why did the forgetful mom buy a treadmill?

She wanted to jog her memory.

Why did the forgetful mom buy a second treadmill?

She forgot she bought the first one!

Child: Dad, would you punish me for something I didn't do?

Dad: Of course not!

Child: Good. Because I didn't clean my room.

How come parents and grandparents were better at history? *There was less of it.*

How are families like fudge?

They're mostly sweet
with a few nuts!

Chapter 4
Get in on the Hi Jinx

Research has shown that laughing might make your brain work better. Laughter helps because it lowers stress. Some scientists have linked laughter to a better memory too. Try laughing at jokes before you study. Maybe your grades will improve!

Take It One Step More

1. Create your own joke about teachers. What are some funny things teachers say or do? Turn it into a joke.

2. **Ask your teachers their favorite jokes. They are sure to have some favorites!**

3. Share the jokes in this book. Which jokes did your classmates find funny? How about the librarian? Your English teacher? Why do you think they found different jokes funny?

GLOSSARY

advice column (ad-VAHYS KOL-uhm)—
an article in a newspaper or magazine that
offers help to people who write in to ask
how to deal with a problem

Congress (KONG-gris)—the chief
lawmaking body in the United States that
is made up of the Senate and the House
of Representatives

declaration (dek-luh-REY-shuhn)—
a document that contains an
official statement

pi (PAHY)—a never-ending number having
a value rounded to eight decimal places
of 3.14159265

stress (STRES)—a state of mental tension
and worry caused by problems in a
person's life or work

BOOKS

Elliott, Rob. *Laugh-Out-Loud Awesome Jokes for Kids.*
Laugh-Out-Loud Jokes for Kids. New York:
HarperCollins, 2017.

Peterson, Megan Cooley. *Pranks to Play on Your
Parents.* Humorous Hi Jinx. Mankato, MN: Black
Rabbit Books, 2018.

Yoe, Craig. *LOL: A Load of Laughs and Jokes for Kids.*
New York: Little Simon, 2017.

WEBSITES

Jokes for Kids
www.activityvillage.co.uk/jokes-for-kids

Kids' Jokes
www.rd.com/jokes/kids/

Teacher Jokes
**www.ducksters.com/jokes/
teachers.php**

INDEX

E

English teachers, 14

F

farts, 6, 7

G

grandparents, 16, 18

H

homework, 15

L

libraries, 12, 13

M

math teachers, 10, 15

P

parents, 17, 18

pi, 10

S

science teachers, 11

social studies teachers, 14